Elgar Country

Peter Sutton

Elgar Country
Peter Sutton
Edited by Black Pear Press

First published in 2022 by Black Pear Press
www.blackpear.net
Copyright © Peter Sutton

ISBN 978-1-913418-60-1

Cover Photograph and Design
by Black Pear Press

Black Pear Press

Preface

These poems are about the composer Sir Edward Elgar and the landscape in which he lived and worked.

He was born in a cottage in Lower Broadheath, a few miles outside Worcester, on 2 June 1857, the fourth of seven children, and the family soon moved to a house by Worcester Cathedral where his father earned a living managing a music shop, tuning pianos, playing the organ at the Catholic Church, and playing second fiddle in the Worcester Glee Club. Young Ted, as he was known, was thus introduced to a wide range of instruments, while from his mother he acquired a lifelong love of poetry.

Initially, he wrote tunes for his family and friends, before composing dances for inmates of the County Asylum and having early work performed in Birmingham and London. Despite being self-taught, in due course he achieved international renown with such works as the *Enigma Variations*, *The Dream of Gerontius*, the *Pomp and Circumstance* marches, and settings of words by over 60 poets.

In his thirties he married one of his mature piano students, who was the daughter of a major-general in the Indian Army and several social rungs above him. They settled in Malvern, and presently took a grander house in Hereford, where Elgar continued to cycle the lanes and draw inspiration from the land. In 1912, they moved to London, where he was never at ease, and during the First World War, which distressed him greatly, he retreated to the Sussex countryside.

After his wife Alice died in 1920, he moved back to Worcester, within sight of the Malvern Hills, and it is often said that their up-and-down outline can be heard in his compositions; he remarked himself that if we hear music on the hills, 'it's only me.' He died on 23 February 1934 and is buried beside Alice on the Malvern Hills.

But we can hear other sounds too on those ancient hills, accumulated over the millennia. Among them will be the words of many writers. The earliest known by name is William

Langland, whose great fourteenth-century poem *Piers Plowman* Elgar called 'a marvellous book...it's my Bible.'

So come to the Malvern Hills, to the counties of Hereford and Worcester, and hear the marvellous words of poets, the sounds of the earth, and the magical music of Elgar.

Contents

The Art of Composition

Let us begin
with a three-note phrase,
an up-up-up
or up-down-up
or up-down-down
or down-down-up,
a four-note phrase,
a five-note phrase,
a one-note minimalinimal phrase,
or any combination,
endless variation,
given the question
how far each time
to jump up-down
and where you begin
and the length of the notes
and the number and nature
of voices and fingers
and blowers and stringers
consorting at once.

The Call

No matter if you cannot say what, when and where:
you need not name the cause,
the argument, the lie,
you need not name the place
where you will go to die.

You need not name the brave
who have answered to the call.
Once they join you in the grave
they will need no names at all,
just time, keep in time, keep in line there.

Music is Memory

Music is memory, parent of poetry,
throbbing in time with the heartbeat of everything,
saying the words that can never be spoken of,
plucked from the sky by our eavesdropping tendencies.

Who was it set out the optimum frequencies,
intervals and mathematical reckonings,
splitting the world into octaves, key signatures,
crotchets and quavers, threnody, rhapsody?

Did they remember our ancestors voicing their
bare-footed challenges, tussles and victories,
tail-turning, lifesaving, breath-holding silences,
hunting cries, birthing pangs, death rattles, agony?

Don't we still dance to the rhythm of venery,
step one-two, stop one-two, pausing to concentrate,
matching the tempo to pace of the enemy,
trotting in time to the speed of the century?

Boots

Boots, boots, boots, boots…
Who is now mon ami, mucker,
vriend, Genosse, moi tovarishch?
Red the common colour flying,
red and something all the banners,
red and nothing all the tatters,
all the rag and bone men, splatters,
all the hanging joints of mutton,
gutted, spitted, turned by potboys,
food for gods of Arcady.

Dulce et decorum bollocks,
Gott mit uns, for King and Country,
Empire, quagmire, Joan of Arc pyre,
martyrs, Tartars, alma maters,
drag 'em out and split 'em lengthways,
right hand cleavers, left hand nosegays,
tread 'em in the common clay.

Brutes, mutes, suits, flutes…
dressed to kill to piercing whistles,
friend and comrade, deadly night raid,
fight for hearth and home and mother,
fight for one thing or another,
fight for nothing but survival,
working order on arrival,
walking dead by oh-six-hundred.
Could they not have asked their god to
spare the sods of Picardy?

Spring Music 1919

The warblers have returned to their old pitch,
the stand of reeds below the Severn bridge.
They come by scores, in bands that fill the air,
and form their twosomes as a prelude to
the rite of spring, their major feast of joy.

They fiddle, plaiting bows with strings of sedge
and strip the willow, plucking sharp new twigs,
repeating every year the same caprice,
each nest a variation on a theme,
arranging it until, content, they rest.

Then with a flourish, movement rocks the nest,
young bell-shaped mouths and drumming, beating wings,
demanding constant trifles on a scale
that strains the parents' love but is the key,
the motive of the yearly roundelay.

The Malvern Hills

Climb to the crook of the Wyche Cutting,
the breezy Worcester Beacon or the British Camp,
and listen and look at the lay of the land,
pillowed and plump and promising lives
of pleasure and leisure the length of the line
like a languorous, listless lizard at rest.

Halt for a moment and you'll hear the hubbub
of palimpsested centuries, of sandals and sneakers,
giants and journeymen, joggers and earls,
mountain bikes, mountebanks, mendicants, monks,
bronze-age bowmen, tobogganers and boffins,
hang-gliders, holy men, hermits and hikers,
conservators, cattlemen, kids with kites,
tourists, centurions, roundheads and tramps,
poets and painters, panthers and pets,
diviners and drovers, donkey-women, druids
celebrating solstices, Samhain and Beltane,
Imbolc and Lughnasadh, looking to the light.

Stand still and you'll see in the scenery below
the plough teams and potteries, quarries and pubs,
cider presses, salt routes, cemeteries, farms,
ironwork and horses and mobile homes,
the hollow-ways, woolpacks, waterworks and woods,
the sanctified springs, the suburbs and towns,
the lorry parks, lime kilns, lords in their keeps,
the rivers and railways, the road works and floods,
the steamers and sails, and motorway signs,
and the trainloads of wounded from war to war,
young men and nurses, yeomanry and Yanks,
in the cockpit of the country, the kingdom, the core.

Malvern Water

Malvern is water,
springs and spouts and riverine lifelines,
snowmelt and rainfall
filtered by memory, granite and lime.

Malvern is healing,
veined and arterial, blue-blooded fault lines,
deep in the jointure,
trickling down through the layers of time.

Malvern is poetry,
thoughts and words still trapped in its bloodlines,
Malvern is music,
matching the wordscape of rhythm and rhyme.

The Healing Hills

Here doctors ordered daily draughts
of Malvern water, wet sheets, walking,
slimming and sitz baths, douches and sluices,
healthy, wholesome, homely living,
amid the modest, mild-mannered shires,
Hereford and Worcester, weathered and warm.

Here Langland penned his poem Piers Plowman,
here Roget arranged his rambling Thesaurus,
here Wordsworth wandered, and Walter de la Mare,
Joseph Cottle, Michael Drayton, Drinkwater, Dyer,
William Bowles, Rupert Brooke and Lizzie Barrett Browning,
C.S. Lewis, C. Day-Lewis and Lascelles Abercrombie,
Harvey, Housman and Auden, Radclyffe Hall,
Edward Thomas, Wilfrid Gibson, Tolkien and Trease,
Siegfried Sassoon and Swinburne and Symonds,
Francis Brett Young, Eleanor Farjeon and Frost,
Shaw and Masefield and many, many more,
and you will be welcomed with a well-spring of words
if you open your eyes and your ears and your mind.

So, pack away your pills and potions,
liniments, salves, elixirs, lotions,
leave the lethal, leaden, gritty,
unclean air of every city.
Come to quiet, country hills
and shrive yourselves of secret ills.

The Source of Music

There is a kindly spirit in the air
that lets the poet and composer place
disordered entrails on an altar where
a friendly muse arranges them with grace.

And sparks from Vulcan's forge, a burning flare,
assist the sanguine hopefuls to evade
the choler, bile and phlegm some artists share,
the meretricious games so often played.

Instead, they hear the truckling, teasing trills
of water gushing forth from clouded hills,
and ancient, urgent, rhythmic, chantry songs
once broadcast from the heights in times of strife
to sounds of reed pipes, bagpipes, drums and gongs,
and buried deep in rock as old as life.

A Song for Elgar

When the moon is fully sixpence and the sky holds back its tears
he still walks the Malverns dreaming of the better, bitter years,
of the notes that clacked like golf-clubs and the frets and keys he
    tapped,
and the five-barred gate on which they swung, the minims that he
    mapped,

looking northward to his childhood, to the spires of hops and
    hope,
to the single, double reeds of Teme,
the four-part songs of home,
and Saint George's and the fancy dress, the crossing and the host,

looking eastward to the Rhineland, to his overture to fame,
long before percussion meant Get down
and nothing stayed the same,
and to London where his friend Herr Jaeger trumpeted his name,

looking westward to America, the gushers and the swells,
and the evensong, the hermits' cells
of Herefordshire hills,
to the lost love and the last love, and the muffled passing bells,

looking southward to the Alpine songs of summer that he set,
to the Sussex woods, the whispered source
of late, too-late quartets,
and the plot where Alice lies, and he would score his endless rest.

Elgar the Composer

Edward set his lover's verses while their hearts yet beat in time,
he and Alice both believing that a poem has to rhyme,
so the air was 'sweetly stirred by the song of bee and bird'
and the sky was always blue, 'deep and rich in every hue'.

Out his music poured like cider, fruity, frothy, pippy part-songs,
instrumental bagatelles and choral hymns and plaintive chansons,
Celtic, Nordic, mythic stories, Sunday morning organ glories,
patriotic taradiddles, works for piano, brass and fiddles.

Melodies came rumbling, tumbling from the clouds like April
    rain,
Pomp and Circumstance, Sea Pictures, Capricieuse, Froissart,
    Cockaigne,
theatre music, deep reflections on the Christian Resurrection,
and sublime but all too human, the Gerontius of Newman.

But the work that brought the greatest, longest, loudest of
    ovations
was the quirky new departure, the Enigma Variations,
fourteen portraits drawn from life of friends, of Edward and his
    wife,
causing future generations endless scholarly frustrations.

A Poetical Symphony

1

This is the   opening   theme of the   symphony
One-two-three   four-five-six   sen-eight-nine   ten-len-twell
whack Tilly   thwack Tilly   rack Tilly   sack Tilly
paa-pa-pa   paa-pa-pa   paa-pa-pa   paa-pa-pa
played with a   zing on the   strings and the   timpani

2

But the next theme is sad and the thunder has ceased
It is free change of key bring your tea come with me
to a feast where you're fleeced by that beast Anna Paest
The bassoon makes you swoon and the drum makes you hum
as you lie in the sun and your soul is released

3

Now they coke it
stroke it troke it
poke it porn it
storm it cornet
stamp it strumpet
tramp it trumpet
mix it stoke it
roll it smoke it
side drum thump it
snare drum clump it
hit so hard the drummer broke it

4

And then again a gentler theme is due
The harp and horn the wind the hawking strings
the whole ensemble plays the tune anew
The oboe sighs and says to all who hear
I am because I am a part of you
And lastly the   opening   upside down   three-two-one

12

sides to the   middle and   played on the   fiddle as
twell-len-ten   six-five-four   nine-eight-sen   my what fun
hoot on the   flute and a   moaning trom——bone and a
bellowing   cello and   eighteen-twelve   bang-crash-gun
The symphony   closes with   one final   choooord
It's over to   you now so   will you ap——plaaaaud?

Enigma

Shall I tell you what it is,
the hidden tune not played by the band
but on which the Variations stand?
Some say it's Mozart or Rule Britannia,
or claim it's some other recycled song,
which is all very clever but quite, quite wrong.

For I'm a joker, don't you see,
a punner and a riddle-setter,
juggling words and jumbling letters,
and the answer's E, that's me.

Write it down, and there I am
when rearranged by Ana Gram:
E N-I then G M-A.

E for Edward Elgar, me.
Turn around the N and I,
and G is G, the key of G,
and there you have it:
E in G.

But, you'll say, there's still M-A,
though if you will pronounce it 'may',
the 'major', not the 'minor' key,
the riddle will be answered for
the whole work starts and ends in G,
minor then major then minor once more,
but the last Variation, named after me,
is ecstatically major throughout; so you see
that here is the answer as plain as day:
E IN G—which one?—MA,
which proves that I'm a major composer
and not an overblown, collegy poser.

And the twist that I find the sweetest and best,

the curious fact which adds to the jest,
is that Alice's military pa,
who rushed the field guns at Kotah,
Sir Henry Gee Roberts, KCB,
was also a major Major-G.

The Malvern Statue

Alight from the train at Great Malvern station,
climb to where Elgar stands dreaming today,
hug him and read the well-tuned dedication.
Alight from the train at Great Malvern station,
see where he's gazing in deep contemplation,
the place where he once taught his pupils to play.
Alight from the train at Great Malvern station,
climb to where Elgar stands dreaming today.

And the Elgar Grave

Visit his grave if you want recreation,
stroll on the Malverns and walk in his tracks,
marvel as he did at Nature's creation.
Visit his grave if you want recreation,
pass by his house on the way from the station,
look out for red commemorative plaques.
Visit his grave if you want recreation,
stroll on the Malverns and walk in his tracks.

The Hereford Statue

In Hereford he stands by his saddle-bagged bicycle
in the claustral calm of the Cathedral close,
straining to hear the settings of psalms,
the evensong offerings of apple-cheeked choristers,
true believers, tradespeople, travellers,
marketing farmers and festival folk;
he's thinking of cycling through somnolent streets
and sinewy, serpentine, sidewinding lanes,
head above hedgerows, catching at harmonies,
swelling with music from storm cloud and skylark,
full-throated fowls and fledgling divas,
the up-and-down liminal lurch of the land,
and quartering cattle the colour of blood.

He listens in silence to the sleepy ensemble
of half-tone echoes from the creeping earth,
impromptu putters from the purling Wye,
tutti that stutter from the tremolo trees,
and the whispering whisht of the westering wind
where he scored more Pomp and Circumstance,
symphonies and songs, a concerto and suites
that speak of sunnier southern days.

Credo

I believe.

I did believe.

In my mother dressed in her Sunday best,
nodding at the sermon,
in my father counting the beats in the pub,
emptying a tankard,
myself like Owl in the balcony
ready to peck at the bellows,
worrying, would he be back in time
to play out the final number?
Hearing him cuss as he climbed the stairs,
sneezing from the snuff.

But in Hereford I lost my faith,
which is not like losing your hat, you know.
The brim had cracked and crumbled to bits
with the tears of grief in Gerontius;
The Apostles, the opening third of a trilogy
teaching the timeless truth of Christ,
saw off the band; and the crown itself
was ripped to shreds when I came to compose
the second surviving part of the set,
the hope of heaven, The Kingdom.

It was not long after he shuffled off,
my death-bed Catholic, not-so-Catholic,
organ-playing father,
and I saw him standing watching me,
toying with his bunch of keys
on the misted green hill.

contd…

Then I looked again and saw
it was not he but, with his key, Saint Peter,
who gathered up the finished score,
stuffed it in his music case
and bicycled unsteadily
away into the drizzle.

And I was bunkered, faithless, done,
hatless in the blazing sun.

A Provincial Composer

Two symphonies and a concerto,
anthems, songs, oratorios,
studies, suites and sonatas,
wind quintets, marches, cantatas,
overtures, hymns and serenades,
knighthood, professorships, accolades,
were no longer enough for an apostate
who'd played in the Powick asylum band
and instructed young ladies in scales,
in spite of his noble transition
to gentleman and a knight of the realm,
and a friend of the Prince of Wales.

He needed, they told him, a leading position,
belonged at the centre of London life
in his opera hat and his tails.
So damned by reflected ambition
he entered the mirrored world of Cockaigne,
where green-eyed falsehood prevails.

London Town

It's a marvellous thing
to be in the swing,
living in smart London town.

I can visit my club,
where I easily rub
shoulders with mitre and gown,

and my music is heard
and I go to absurd
dinners in fashionable squares.

But what I write's wrong,
just the odd little song;
I'm missing the apples and pears,

the orchards and fields
with their sweet-scented yields,
the hills with a hint of the wild,

the lowing from byres,
the canonical choirs,
the sounds that I knew as a child.

The war puts an end;
I no longer pretend
to laugh at society's games,

though they borrow my tunes
to inspire new platoons
to add to the long list of names.

1914

He had set words when they were wooden toys,
when life was resurrected every spring,
when birds and bees were ever on the wing,
and foreign fields meant harmless summer joys.

Then autumn threshing was the loudest noise,
then love meant silent, patient suffering,
then innocence was still the modish thing,
and subalterns were careless bluecoat boys,

But now he saw all rhyme and reason fail,
the people spoke in leaden, trudging prose
and spat out phrases hard as winter hail,
as uniform, as harsh and bellicose,
as mutilating, bruising, brutish, curt,
and music could alone convey his hurt.

Diminuendo

He fled to ancient, fragrant Sussex woods,
where autumn fires and wood smoke stroked the air
deranged by distant strains of cordite hell,
and ponds and cisterns could not slake the thirst.

He walked the woodways, kicking at the tilth
that fades in death to earth and saw the monks
now turned, old custom said, to rustling trees
no longer chanting plainsong to the skies.

He wrote and wrote, for orchestra and strings.
The cello was his soldier's weeping voice,
percussion aped the shouting of the guns,
and brass proclaimed a stumbling, wordless march.

And when the snare-drum stopped its gallows trap,
his Alice, his first subject, faltered, died,
and tuneless, muddy monotones, pitch-dark,
marched out of time across discordant lines.

To Worcester he returned, to Severnside,
where part-songs mouthed the plaint of lonely reeds
and woodwind, brass and organ softly played
a slow, unfinished piano serenade.

The Worcester Statue

And now here I stand in my robes in apparent repose
outside the Cathedral where fame was my childhood desire,
across from the shop and the house where I learnt to compose,
to dream and aspire.

I harvested tunes from the air, the earth, water and fire,
and I have returned to the city, the home that I chose,
to listen for ever to concert and organ and choir.

You will still hear music surrounding me when the wind blows,
for though I am muted, the generous muse will not tire.
She'll be there beside you till time shall run backwards and close;
she yet shall inspire.

Worcester

Bustling, hustling,
outwork, piecework,
glove works, steel works,
coal yards, stockyards,
factors, tractors,
sauces, horses,
bookies, rookies,
bowlers, strollers,
wagons, flagons,
brewers, hewers,
lawyers, sawyers,
guildhall, football,
medicine, porcelain,
highways, low ways,
railways, waterways,
house of varieties,
friendly societies,
pubs, clubs
and cricket.
And in the midst,
the Cathedral.

Music in the Air

Sir Edward Elgar's music haunts the reeds,
the bracken, willows, bluebells, birch and gorse
of Malvern's hills and Severn's silted shore,
the land where it was made and it belongs.
And you as well may pluck tunes from the air:
you only need to listen and to look,
to hear and see, your senses sharp, alert,
and you will catch the musings of the earth.

For music is intrinsic, in-built, rife,
inscribed upon the heavens like the stars,
the rainbowed arc, the thunder and the clouds,
the budding storm, the dew and falling tears.
It makes the body tingle, ache with pain,
it takes your breath away and strikes you dumb,
and no words you can utter will convey
the ecstasy and sorrow of its ways.

So let your life and loves walk hand in hand
with echoes of its elemental voice,
and follow as it changes mood and key,
explores new themes, abandons them and seeks
for more and ever more from out the sky,
the rising, falling heartbeat of the land.
Preserve the sounds, the melodies you hear
and press them, keep them, share them, hold them dear.

The Worcester Races

They're cantering down the course to the start,
Concertina looking sprightly,
Ocarina and Jazz-twice-nightly,
Clarinet and Cream-cornett,
Piccolo and Soft-and-low.

They're turning and forming a well-tempered line,
Flugelhorn tootling off, being awkward,
being brought back, the squad moving forward,
and now they are under starter's orders.
He's checking and raising his arm and—they're off!

And it's First-violin that moves into the lead,
First-violin from What's-the-thing-in,
then Xylophone and Dog-and-bone,
a length ahead of Carillon,
Carillon, Clarion and Just-play-on.

And over the reeds it is First-violin,
with Carillon, Clarion and Just-play-on,
then Xylophone and Dog-and-bone,
Flageolet and Missing-fret,
Glockenspiel and Easy-peal.

The leaders are into a regular rhythm,
an upbeat, rollicking algorithm,
the rest strung out in a straggly line,
with Bagpipe trailing and Auld-lang-syne,
Caterwaul, Catcall and Dead-march-from-Saul.

They shimmy now left and right through the Serpent,
some jostling there, some unwanted movement,
Solo and Part-song involved in a ding-dong,
Banjo content to play second fiddle,

Baritone-sax more or less in the middle.

Sousaphone's moving up fast on the rail
Enough-to-waken-the-dead on her tail.
but as they quick waltz around Plectrum Corner,
it's First-violin from Mandolin,
then Clarinet, Spinet and fifth, Boxed-set.

As they come to the water still First-violin,
but as they go over, she stumbles, she's in!
First-violin's in the water, a faller!
One moment she's sawing her way through the air
and the next, she's flat out and no longer a player.

And now with no leader it's utter confusion:
concussion, contusion, scratched heads in profusion,
Mandolin's battered, Spinet's leg is shattered,
Box-set has landed head first, badly tattered,
Clarinet's croaked and the whole field has scattered.

But Squeezebox has wriggled out clear of the wreck,
Squeezebox, Bandoneon and Piano-accordion,
this trio leading the field neck and neck,
from Quartertone, Conch, Penny-whistle, Antiphony,
Squeak-plonk and Tone-deaf, Twelve-tone, Cacophony.

And as they turn into the Bombardon Straight
Squeak-plonk is challenging, scraping past Melody.
And Timpani's making a sudden late run for it,
belting along, going hammer and tongs at it,
through the Kazoo and the Eight-bar Gate.

But now Pianola's outpacing him, chasing him,
little legs going hell's bells like two piston-rods,
anyone's guess now, it's up to the gods,
she's an amateur rider, a real outsider,   contd…

29

one of the also-rans, longest of odds.

And at the last post Pianola beats Timpani
by a short head from Squeak-plonk and Melody.
Pianola comes first with a final short burst
that astounded the punters, was nearly too late,
and outplayed the rest in the Elgar Gold Plate.

The Railway

The train still trickles from Worcester to Hereford,
sometimes on time and not seldom behind,
pausing at Malvern and Colwall and Ledbury,
no longer waiting on long-ago lines
from Bromyard and Leominster and Gloucester and Tewkesbury,
through vanished halts at Saint Johns and at Bransford,
at Newland, the Wells, Stoke Edith for Tarrington,
at Ashperton and at the marshes of Withington,
still pouring smuts from its uppity funnels,
lifting its skirts in a pit-a-pat flurry,
hooting at bats in the Malvern Hills tunnel,
single line now, come along, we must scurry.

Look as you pass at the lingering landscape,
woods where windflowers, gorse and woodruff,
bluebells, bellflowers, bracken and ramsons,
hatstands of ash and birch and hawthorn,
hard-hearted oak and haloes of holly,
bludgeons of blackthorn and handcuffs of brambles
wave and wonder at why there's a hurry.
See the red earth with its hundred home harvests,
bushels of wheat and bearded barley,
hoppers of hops and oats and apples,
pears as heavy and hard as armour,
goosegogs and greens and grapes for new wine.

The Old Line

As we explore the old iron-bed tracks,
stumbling over familiar roots,
fingering copper-plate names on the trees,
remembering branches cut down in the mud,
conjuring black and white outlines of men
waltzing with women in evergreen frocks,
counting the decades, the children, the pence,
feeling the bark and the sap of our youth,
touching the friable paper-thin leaves
floating to earth at the close of the day,
hearing the lingering rattle and din,
hoping perhaps to lay down a new line
blazing a permanent way to the stars,
the down signal shows us we are at the end.

Reviews

'Let us begin'—the opening words of this latest collection by Peter Sutton hang in the air with the anticipation of a conductor's baton held aloft, poised to take us on an exhilarating journey through the musical majesty of Edward Elgar via a 'wordscape of rhythm and rhyme'. By turns playful and poignant, Sutton's poems dance with flair and grace across the pages, illuminating the life and times of this singular composer with a joyful sense of passion and warmth. A true virtuoso, Sutton makes the most of poetic devices, creating a 'well-spring of words' that carry their own sound, movement and musical delight. *Elgar Country* is a captivating collection, written by a poet who intuitively understands the Malvern land where Elgar's music was made and belongs.
—*Sara-Jane Arbury, poet, playwright, and performer*

The Malvern Hills are at the high centre of Elgar Country: they've been 'palimpsested' by many artistic talents and Peter Sutton's poems lay down another evocative layer. They are a guide-book, an examination of the inspiration, and a poetic score to what the area has meant to so many, not least Elgar himself. No better place to read the poems than high on the ridge of those 'pillowed and plump' Hills, overlooking Elgar Country; and through the poems, understanding the heart of our own and Elgar's muse.
—*David Armitage, Assistant Partnership Manager, Malvern Hills AONB*

If Elgar's music with its quintessential Englishness can stir the soul, Peter Sutton's poetry about the great man and his relationship with the Worcestershire countryside will set it spinning. These poems are full of rhythm and cadence, precision, and energy. There is laugh-aloud humour in *The Worcester Races*, a complete history in *The Malvern Hills*, the celebration of *Spring Music 1919*, and an explanation of the magic in *The Source of Music*.

This is a feel-good collection, and the poet's warmth and wit breathe through every page.
—*Alison Chisholm, poet*

In Elgar Country, poet Peter Sutton takes us through some of the significant events, places and artistic landmarks of Elgar's life. Sutton's verse often peeks through the public persona of the man and reveals some of the underlying passions that drove him to write some of the our best loved music. Those readers who know and love Elgar's music will recognise many allusions to his works and what influenced and inspired him to write them. The themes of childhood, Worcester, the Malvern Hills and the Great War that so disturbed his creative output are ever present. To those new to Elgar and his world, these poems will stand as a platform from which to understand how a creative genius takes his inspiration from his surroundings.
—*Stuart Freed, Acting Chairman of the Elgar Society*

Peter Sutton imparts tremendous knowledge of composer and county as he draws together many threads of Elgar's life. In this collection love, loss, the passing of time and place all play pinnacle roles, giving a deep exploration of family, Alice, and Elgar's work. Sutton is an engaging writer, consistently sensitive as both biographer and poet, his insight into Elgar's life is revealing and described so vividly you will see it for yourself.

In *A Song for Elgar* Sutton manages to incorporate an entire history. His wordplay becomes a musical score, *Elgar Country* captures his evident enjoyment of craft.

A delightful rich study of Elgar and the landscape of his life. A thoroughly compelling read.
—*Nina Lewis, Worcestershire Poet Laureate (2017-18)*

The collection of Elgarian delights contains 27 poems whose sharply focused images are both entertaining and erudite. Ranging from the playful parlance of *Worcester* to the deeper *Music in the Air* and puzzling *Enigma*, we journey through Peter Sutton's

unique insights into the composer's life and work, and his beloved countryside.
—*Peter Smith, Artistic Director, Autumn in Malvern Festival*

There is more than one country in Peter Sutton's absorbing sequence. He brings to almost tangible life the byways of Elgar's beloved Worcestershire. But there is also that inner land of Elgar's music and its inspirations, be they the jostle of folk, past and present, on the Malvern Hills ('giants and journeymen, joggers and earls') or the 'woodways' of Sussex, when 'He wrote and wrote, for orchestra and strings.' And there is the land of music as memory, compelling us to 'dance to the rhythm of venery, / step one-two, stop one-two...' Music pervades these poems: so do poignancy, humour, the poet's sheer love of his subject. Sutton hasn't simply honoured Wolverhampton Wanderers' most august fan from the outside. His is an emphatically inward eye. Elgar set the work of many poets to music. Compellingly, Sutton has set the composer to words.
Michael W. Thomas, poet, author, 'TLS' reviewer, lecturer at The Open University

Thanks

It was the late Catherine Moody who first sparked my interest in Elgar by suggesting that I write the play *Elgar and Alice* to mark the composer's 150th anniversary in 2007. This I did, with the generous assistance of the Norbury family. Katrina Norbury, now sadly deceased, co-produced the play, helped to research it, and acted in it alongside Janet Hargreaves, Joy McBrinn and Gerald Harper, who drew on his distinguished career to tell me not what to write, but what I should not have written. The director Gene David Kirk gave me further advice, and I am indebted to Chris Jaeger, then Artistic Director of the Swan Theatre, Worcester, for taking up the play and hosting the premiere.

Ever since then, members of the Elgar Society, guest speakers, and the staff of the Elgar Birthplace, now 'The Firs' managed by the National Trust, have sustained and expanded my knowledge of the composer and his life and work, and have facilitated further research. Hilary Elgar has also given me unstinting friendly encouragement.

As for Langland and the Malvern Hills, the late Gwen Appleby took a group of local writers up on the hills some years ago to show us where the poet had his vision. She spoke so lovingly that I was moved to offer a presentation about him to the 2012 Autumn in Malvern Festival, and I am grateful to Peter Smith, Director of the Festival, for accepting the proposal. My modern verse translation of the entire text was then published in 2014 by McFarland of North Carolina.

The helpful and obliging people involved in these projects are too numerous to name, while my poetic skills, such as they are, have been hugely improved by members of such groups as Accent on Poetry, the 'Hereabouts' Herefordshire Stanza, Ledbury Poetry Festival Salons, Worcester LitFest Speakeasy, Malvern Writers' Circle, and the Worcester Libraries Poetry Bubble. My thanks go out to all of them.

I would also like to thank Black Pear Press for their confidence in the present collection, in particular Polly Stretton for her detailed and sympathetic editing, and my reviewers for their kind words.

About the Author

Peter Sutton is joint winner of the 2021 Kipling Society John McGivering Poetry Prize, and began his poetry career in 2014 with publication by McFarland of North Carolina of his modern alliterative verse translation of William Langland's 7500-line medieval poem *Piers Plowman*. This was followed in 2019 by the publication of *Poems of Armenian War and Peace*, jointly written with Liana Hayrapetyan and sponsored by an Armenian cultural trust, and some 30 other poems have appeared in the journals *Acumen*, *HQ*, *Orbis*, *Poetry Salzburg Review* and *Sarasvati*, online or in anthologies.

Peter has given readings from his *Piers Plowman* and other work at conferences and poetry festivals in the US and the UK, and he frequently appears at West Midlands poetry events.

His plays *Elgar and Alice* and *The Prebumptious Mr Punch* were premiered in Worcester, in 2007 and 2013 respectively, and his translation from German of Rolf Hochhuth's *Death of a Hunter* was first seen in London in 2018.

Peter has edited and translated numerous books, articles and reports for international organisations, lawyers, and arts centres, and is a former Head of Publications at the UNESCO Institute for Education in Hamburg. He has written and spoken widely on languages, Elgar, Langland, and poetry, has written German language textbooks, and has been a visiting lecturer at universities in Armenia, Germany, Russia and the UK.

For more see his website www.petersutton.uk